Aberdeenshire

COUNCIL

Aberdeenshire Libraries
www.aberdeenshire.gov.uk/libraries
Renewals Hotline 01224 661511

3 1 MAY 2016

HQ

1 5 NOV 2016

ABERDEENSHIRE
LIBRARIES

WITHDRAWN
FROM LIBRARY

Aberdeenshire

3173838

CLASSIFICATION
AND
EVOLUTION

Peter Riley

W
FRANKLIN WATTS
LONDON•SYDNEY

To my granddaughter, Tabitha Grace.

First published in Great Britain in 2015 by The Watts Publishing Group

Copyright text © Peter Riley 2015
All rights reserved.

Editor: Julia Bird
Designer: Mo Choy

Photo acknowledgments: Andre Anita/Shutterstock: 13c. Anoliso/Dreamstime: 7b. Stephane Bidouze/Shutterstock: 13t. Todd Boland/Shutterstock: 8br. Evgenia Bolyukh/Shutterstock: 19t. (kittens sleeping) Yuriy Boyko/Shutterstock: 17cl. Willyam Bradbury/Shutterstock: 3, 11t. Greg Brave/Shutterstock: 6b. Butterfly Hunters/Shutterstock: 4, 31r. Steve Byland/Shutterstock: 29b. cbpix/Shutterstock: 12t. Roderick Chen, All Canada Photos/Alamy: 22t. Opas Chotiphantawanon/Shutterstock: 10bl. Classic Image/Alamy: 29c. Denise Alison Coyle/Shutterstock: 15t. dreamerb/Shutterstock: 6t. Mikhail Dudarev/Shutterstock: 5b. Melinda Fawver/Shutterstock: 17cr. Fotokostic/Shutterstock: 9b. fusebulb/Shutterstock: 6t. Ulrike Haberkorn/Shutterstock: 29t. Amy Nicole Harris/Shutterstock: 15b. Martin Harvey/Alamy: 21b. Mark Higgins/Shutterstock: 22b. Nataliya Hora/Shutterstock: 5t. javaman/Shutterstock: 29t. Tory Kallman/Shutterstock: 14b. Kamnuan/Shutterstock: 14t, 16br. Lev Kropotov/Shutterstock: 25b. Ivan Kuzmin/Shutterstock: 21tl. Hugh Lansdown/Shutterstock: 13b. Leene/Shutterstock: 24. Luis Loro/Shutterstock: 18c. Luminate Photos by Judith/Shutterstock: 21tr. arek malang/Shutterstock: 18b. manfredxy/Shutterstock: 28. Alfredo Marquez/Shutterstock: 12b. Astrid & Hanns Frieder Michler/SPL: 7t. NagyDodo/Shutterstock: front cover, 1. Nazzu/Shutterstock: 20t. NHM/Alamy: 23t. Michal Ninger/Shutterstock: 25tr. patjo/Shutterstock: 11b. Dmitry Pichugin/Shutterstock: 20b. Maryna Pieshkun/Shutterstock: 10tr. Olga Popova/Shutterstock: 17bl. JC Revy/ISM/SPL: 25cl. Mauro Rodrigues/Shutterstock: 16bl. Sombra/Shutterstock: 2, 23c. Ryszard Steimachowicz/Dreamstime: 8l. Artur Synenko/Shutterstock: 17br. Tanor/Shutterstock: 19 Adrian Thomas/SPL: 26b. Bildagentur Zoonar GmbH/Shutterstock: 9t.

Every attempt has been made to clear copyright. Should there be any inadvertent omission please apply to the publisher for rectification.

ISBN 978 1 4451 3510 6

Dewey number: 591

Printed in China

Franklin Watts
An imprint of
Hachette Children's Group
Part of The Watts Publishing Group
Carmelite House
50 Victoria Embankment
London EC4Y 0DZ

An Hachette UK Company
www.hachette.co.uk

www.franklinwatts.co.uk

ABERDEENSHIRE LIBRARIES	
3173838	
Bertrams	16/09/2015
J570.12	£12.99

FSC
www.fsc.org
MIX
Paper from responsible sources
FSC® C104740

Contents

Classifying living things

There are over eight million different kinds of living thing on the Earth. Scientists arrange them into groups to make them easier to study. This process of putting living things into groups is called classifying.

❚ How could you arrange these moth and butterflies into groups?

4

PLANTS, ANIMALS AND MICROORGANISMS

All living things have seven features which are called the characteristics of life. These are feeding, respiration (releasing energy), movement, growth, reproduction, excretion (getting rid of waste) and sensitivity. The three major groups of living things are plants, animals and microorganisms. It is easy to separate the first two groups from the last because you do not need a microscope to see them. Plants are separated from animals by two substances that they make – cellulose and chlorophyll. Cellulose is the supporting substance in roots and shoots. Chlorophyll is the green pigment that gives leaves their colour. Plants use it to collect the energy in sunlight for making food.

❚ The chlorophyll in these leaves absorbs the energy in sunlight to make food for the tree.

THE KINGDOMS OF LIVING THINGS

The plant and animal groups are also known as the plant and animal kingdoms. The microorganism group, also known as microbes, has three kingdoms. They are the Monera, which includes bacteria and blue-green algae, the Protoctista, which have bodies made from single cells, and fungi, which includes moulds and toadstools. Although many fungi can be seen, they all have a stage in their life cycle when they are microscopic.

❚ These toadstools are classified as fungi.

HOW TO CLASSIFY

The first step in classifying living things is to look at their features, such as legs, wings, petals or leaves. The next step is to compare the features of the living things. This is done in two ways:

- By looking at how two living things are different, for example one may have leaves and the other may have fins.
- By looking at how two living things are similar, for example do they have the same number of legs and wings?

Living things which have similar features are put in the same group. Living things which are different are put in different groups.

INVESTIGATE

Collect 20 pictures of living things by taking photos, cutting pictures from a magazine or downloading from the Internet. Use the steps in classifying to sort them into groups.

Microbes

All living things are made of cells. An adult human body is made up of about 37 trillion cells. Microbes such as those in the Monera and Protoctista groups have a body made from just one cell, while fungi also have a similar one cell stage in their life cycle.

MONERA

Monera do not have a control centre called a nucleus in their cells. Their kingdom is divided into two groups – blue-green algae and bacteria. Blue-green algae can live on their own, but they may also form threads or clumps of cells surrounded by jelly. They make their own food, like plants, in a process called photosynthesis. They form the plankton in oceans, seas and lakes. Bacteria have three types of body shape – round, rod-shaped or coiled. Most bacteria feed on the remains of living things or their wastes. They can be found almost everywhere. Some types of bacteria can cause disease. One example is the salmonella bacteria which causes food poisoning.

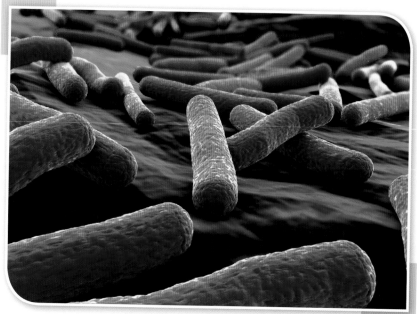

▮ The E.coli bacteria is found in the intestines of many living things. Most forms of E.coli are harmless, but some can make you very ill.

▮ Huge numbers of microscopic threads of blue-green algae have coloured the surface of this lake.

PROTOCTISTA

Protoctista microbes have cells with a nucleus. They are found in aquatic habitats and inside other living things. There are three main types. One type can change their shape and move by letting their insides flow into their new shape. They feed on particles of food. Some can cause disease. A second type has a fixed shape and a long hair which it uses like a whip to move it through water. It makes its own food like a plant. The third type has a fixed shape covered with many tiny hairs which wave to and fro to move the body through the water. They feed on particles of food.

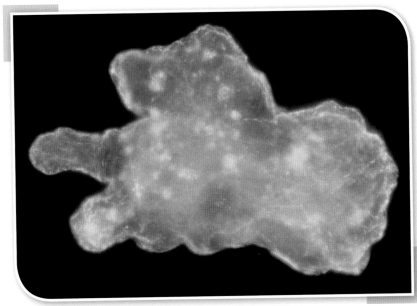

❚ This member of the Protoctista is called an amoeba. You can see its pink circular nucleus and its arms pushing out to take up a new shape.

FUNGI

Fungi can be found in soil, damp food, inside living things and in aquatic habitats. Fungi make cells called spores to reproduce. This is the single cell stage in their life cycle. When a spore opens, a thread grows out which begins to feed on any dead plant and animal material it can find. Over time a network of threads form which may produce a stalk and cap we call a toadstool or mushroom. Some fungi, called yeasts, have single-celled bodies all their lives.

❚ A network of fungal threads have fed on the wood in this log and produced toadstools.

VIRUSES

Viruses are microscopic but they are not classified as living things as they do not have all the seven characteristics of life. They simply reproduce when they get inside the cells of other living things, where they can cause disease.

INVESTIGATE

Put the cap (top) of an open mushroom on a sheet of white paper. Make sure it has its gills downwards, facing the paper. Leave overnight and look for any spores that have fallen from the gills.

Plants

Plants do not show the characteristics of life (see page 5) as clearly as animals. However, they do release energy through respiration, excrete carbon dioxide, are sensitive to their surroundings by moving and growing towards light and reproduce using spores and seeds. The plant kingdom is divided into five major groups.

Seaweeds' holdfasts helps secure it to rocky shores.

ALGAE

Most algae have bodies of one cell, though some form groups of cells in the shape of threads or balls. The biggest algae are seaweeds. These have a holdfast that is used to grip onto rocks and a leaf-like structure called a frond which may be coloured green, red or brown. This makes food like the leaves in other kinds of plants. Some microscopic algae join with fungi to form crusty structures on rocks and branches called lichens.

LIVERWORTS AND MOSSES

Plants in this group do not have proper roots. They have threads which hold them onto the ground or to rocks. They are often found in damp, shady places. Liverworts have flat green pads rather than leaves. Mosses have tiny stems and leaves and grow together in groups that may be shaped like mats or cushions. All members of this group reproduce by making spores.

Mosses and liverworts grow stalks above them to help them make and spread spores.

FERNS

Ferns have roots, stems and feathery leaves called fronds. They reproduce by making spores in patches on the underside of their fronds.

CONIFERS

Conifers are shrubs or trees that have roots and woody stems. Most have needle-like leaves which are green all year round (known as evergreen). They reproduce by making seeds inside cones. The cones open to release the winged seeds into the air.

❚ These open pine cones are ready to release their seeds.

FLOWERING PLANTS

Flowering plants have roots, stems and leaves. Some flowering plants have woody stems and grow into trees and bushes, but most are not woody and have stems that die before winter. All have flowers that produce fruits and seeds.

❚ The trees in this photo have woody stems (trunks). The flowering plants below them have non-woody stems.

INVESTIGATE

Algae may form green patches on tree trunks. Look at tree trunks and find some. Which sides of a trunk do they grow on – north, south, east or west? Use a compass to find out. Can you link your results to the direction from which wet weather comes?

Animals – invertebrates

The animal kingdom is divided into two groups. Vertebrates have a skeleton made of bone and cartilage. Invertebrates do not have this kind of skeleton. Over 97 per cent of all animals on the Earth are invertebrates.

WORMS

This group of invertebrates is divided into three subgroups. All have tube-like bodies supported by water and no legs. The flatworms are small worms with flat bodies. Over half of flatworms are parasites, meaning that they live in a host animal and feed off it. The roundworms have long, thin bodies and can be microscopic or several centimetres long. Some live as parasites, but many live in the soil. The annelid worms have long, thin bodies divided into segments. Annelid worms are found in water habitats and damp soil.

❙ Earthworms are annelids. They mix up soil by burrowing into it and help to make it fertile.

ARTHROPODS

Arthropods all have a tough, protective covering called an exoskeleton. The exoskeleton has joints in it that allow the animal to move. Arthropods are divided into four subgroups. These are:
- insects (six legs)
- spiders (eight legs)
- centipedes and millipedes (30 legs or more)
- crustaceans. These have a shell-type skeleton, as seen in crabs and shrimps.

MOLLUSCS

Members of the mollusc group have soft, unsegmented bodies that are internally supported by water. Many, such as snails, have shells in which they can hide from predators, while others, such as squid, have tentacles which they use to attract and catch prey.

❙ Crabs have a thick shell or exoskeleton made of a mineral called calcium carbonate

▌Many jellyfish can deliver a painful sting with their tentacles.

JELLYFISH

Members of this group have a soft disk-shaped, bell-shaped or cylindrical body that is supported by water. Their mouth is surrounded by tentacles.

STARFISH

Members of the starfish group have tough spiny skin. They have at least five arms and many tube-shaped feet. Some types of starfish, such as sea urchins, are shaped like a ball.

INVESTIGATE

Look for invertebrates around your home or school. Identify the group to which each one belongs. Keep a tally chart of the different animals you find. Which is the most common group of invertebrates in your chart?

▌Starfish can be seen along the shoreline and are often found in rockpools.

Animals – vertebrates

Vertebrates are animals which have a skeleton of bone and cartilage inside their body. There are five major groups of vertebrates.

I Sharks are classed as vertebrates because they have a skeleton made of bendy cartilage.

FISH

Fish have fins and most have skin covered with small, tough plates called scales. They can breathe underwater through structures called gills and almost all fish are coldblooded. There are two major subgroups of fish – those with a skeleton of cartilage, such as sharks and rays, and those with a skeleton of bone, such as cod and haddock.

AMPHIBIANS

Amphibians include frogs, toads, salamanders and newts. They all have smooth, slimy skin and a life cycle which features a tadpole stage in water. The adult stage lives on land, usually in damp habitats. All amphibians are coldblooded. Newly hatched tadpoles have gills to breathe underwater, but adult amphibians have lungs and can also breathe through their slimy skin.

I A frog's slimy skin can take in oxygen and release carbon dioxide.

REPTILES

There are four subgroups of reptiles: crocodiles and alligators, turtles and tortoises, lizards and snakes. Snakes are the only reptile group without legs. Reptiles are almost all coldblooded and their skin is covered in scales. They breathe through lungs. Most female reptiles lay soft-shelled eggs, though some snakes give birth to live young.

❚ Snakes can be found in the sea, as well as on land.

❚ Penguins are flightless birds. They use their wings as flippers for swimming.

BIRDS

Birds are warmblooded. They have bodies covered in feathers and wings that most use to fly. The females lay hard-shelled eggs.

INVESTIGATE

Use books and the Internet to find out which major vertebrate groups are found in tropical rainforests, mountains, deserts, woodlands and near the north and south poles.

MAMMALS

All mammals are warmblooded and have hair on their body at some stage in their life cycle. Female mammals also produce milk to feed their young. There are three subgroups of mammals. The egg-laying group includes only three mammals: the duck-billed platypus and two species of spiny anteater. The marsupial group is much larger. The females in this group have a pouch in which they rear their young. Kangaroos, opossums and koalas are all marsupials. Placental mammals make up the largest group. The females of this group have an organ called a uterus inside them in which the very young mammal develops. The baby is connected to the uterus by a placenta which provides it with nourishment until it is born.

❚ The spiny anteater is an egg-laying mammal.

Classification

Scientists sort the living things in each kingdom into a series of groups so that they can be identified precisely. Words made up from Latin and Greek are used in classification. These words are used by all scientists worldwide so there is no confusion over the identity of a living thing.

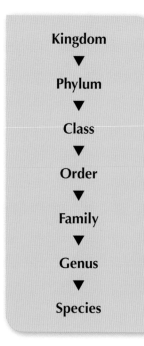

Kingdom
▼
Phylum
▼
Class
▼
Order
▼
Family
▼
Genus
▼
Species

▌Dolphins belong to the order Cetacea.

PHYLUM

First the living things in a kingdom are sorted into groups according to a few major features. Each of these groups is called a phylum. For example, in the animal kingdom animals with an exoskeleton and jointed legs are placed in the phylum Arthropoda. Animals with a tube running along their back that gives them support are placed in a phylum called Chordata. The African bush elephant, for example, belongs to the phylum Chordata.

CLASS

Each phylum is divided into classes. The phylum Chordata, for example, has five major classes – fish, amphibians, reptiles, birds and mammals. The African bush elephant belongs to the class Mammalia.

ORDER

Each class is divided up further into orders. The mammal class, for example, is divided into 26 orders. The African bush elephant belongs to the order Proboscidea.

▌This centipede is placed in the phylum Arthropoda.

FAMILY

Each order is divided further into families. The African bush elephant belongs to the family Elephantidae.

GENUS

Each family is divided into smaller groups. Each of these is called a genus (plural genera). The African bush elephant belongs to the genus Loxidonta.

SPECIES

Each genus is divided into species – the smallest classification group. Animals and plants of the same species share the same characteristics and can reproduce together. The African elephant genus Loxodonta, for example, is divided into two species – the bush elephant (Loxodonta africana) and the forest elephant (Loxodonta cyclotis).

❙ The tiger belongs to the genus Panthera.

CARL LINNAEUS

Swedish scientist Carl Linnaeus (1707–1778) was the first to use generic and species names to identify living things. These Latin and Greek words describe features of the living thing. For example the scientific name for the African clawed toad is Xenopus leavis. The generic name Xenopus is made up from two Greek words – 'xenos' meaning strange and 'pus' meaning foot. This refers to the frog having claws on three of its toes, which is unusual for amphibians. The specific name laevis is Latin for smooth and refers to the animal's smooth skin.

❙ The African bush elephant's scientific name is Loxodonta africana.

INVESTIGATE

Find the scientific name for a human, cat, dog, sheep and horse.

Identification keys

When most people want to identify a plant or animal they look for a picture of it in a book or on the Internet. When ecologists are identifying living things in a habitat they use an identification key. There are two kinds of key – a numbered key and a branching key.

THE NUMBERED KEY

A numbered key helps you to identify something by asking a series of questions. The questions are usually arranged in pairs. When you have read each question you look at the plant or animal you are trying to identify and find an answer. The answer is simply yes or no. When you have answered in this way, the key guides you to the next pair of questions and you read and look again. Going through the key in this way leads you to the identity of the living thing.

A NUMBERED KEY FOR COMMON INVERTEBRATES

1   Animal with a soft body and no legs .... see **2**
    Animal with a hard body and legs........................... see **4**

2   Animal with a long body with rings....................... earthworm
    Animal with a long body and no rings.................... see **3**

3   Animal with a shell on its back.............................. snail
    Animal without a shell on its back........................ slug

4   Animal with more than fourteen pairs of legs .... see **5**
    Animal with less than fourteen pairs of legs .... see **6**

5   Animal with a flat brown or yellow body................centipede
    Animal with a black or dark pink body...................millipede

6   Animal with seven pairs of legs .... woodlouse
    Animal with less than seven pairs of legs .... see **7**

7   Animals with four pairs of legs .... spider
    Animals with three pairs of legs .... insect

▌A woodlouse has a hard exoskeleton and seven pairs of legs.

A BRANCHING KEY

In a branching key you start in the centre at the top and read the pair of features in the first two branches. You look at the plant or animal you are trying to identify and decide which feature you can see. You then read the pair of features further down the branch and look at the living thing again and so on until you identify it. Branching keys are shorter than the numbered keys because they take up much more space.

A TREE LEAF KEY

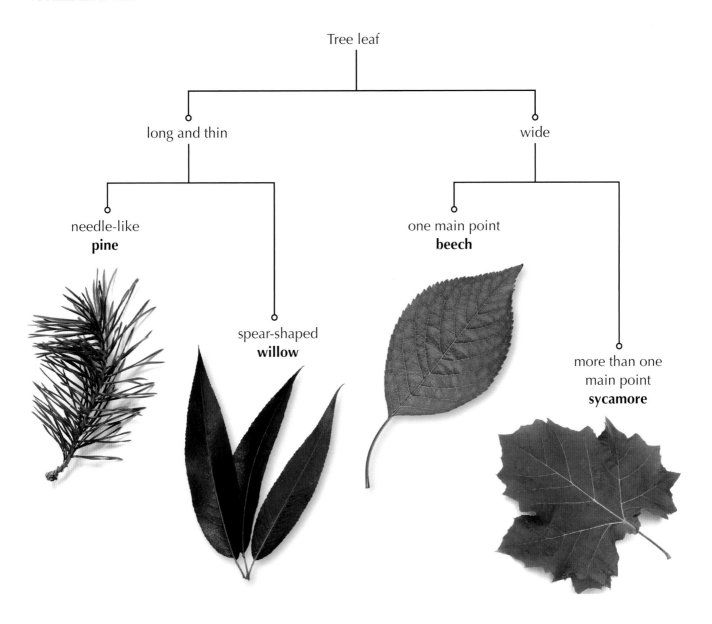

INVESTIGATE

Find pictures of an ant, fly, butterfly and spider. Can you make a numbered key and a branching key to identify them?

Variation

If you look at the members of any one species you will find that they have features which are slightly different from each other. These features that vary among the members of a species are called variations.

VARIATION IN HUMANS

There are many variations in the human species. These include height, weight, skin colour, hair colour, eye colour, freckles, straight hair, curly hair, ear lobes that are attached to the side of the neck and earlobes that are not attached to the side of the neck.

VARIATION IN FAMILIES

When family photographs are studied, certain similarities and differences can be seen between family members. Some variations, such as shape of face, nose or the colour of the hair may be seen in a child, its parent and even its grandparent. This suggests that variations pass from one generation to another. It also suggests that the variations get mixed up as they do this (see page 19).

❙ Features such as the same eye shape may be seen in different generations.

These kittens show variation in fur colour and pattern.

PASSING ON VARIATIONS

Most plants and animals produce a new generation by sexual reproduction. For this to take place, a male and female's sex cells (gametes) are fused together in a process called fertilisation. In each sex cell there are a set of instructions for making a new individual. These instructions are called genes. When a living thing makes sex cells it mixes up the genes and supplies each gamete with half the genes that are needed. When fertilisation occurs, the two gametes form a cell called a zygote which has a complete set of instructions that are slightly different from each parent. This leads to variation being seen as the new individual grows up.

INVESTIGATE

What variations have been selected to produce different breeds of dogs? Describe three examples.

BREEDING LIVING THINGS

People have been breeding living things for their special features for centuries. Plant breeders, for example, select plants with variations such as large, bright petals and breed them together. This can produce a generation of plants with even larger and brighter petals.

These plants have been bred to produce flowers with many large petals.

Adapting to a habitat

The climate and landscape of the different places on the Earth produce different habitats. The living things in each habitat survive because as a group they have adapted to the conditions there. The features which help a living thing adapt to its habitat are called adaptations. This spread looks at adaptations in an African grassland habitat.

▌ Grassland habitats support many grazing animals.

GRASSLAND ADAPTATIONS: BODY

The mammals that live on the grasslands of Africa have many adaptations to their habitat. The stripes of the zebra help to hide it away from lions in the tall grass. The giraffe has long legs and neck so that it can eat leaves in the treetops and does not have to compete with the other grassland herbivores for food. Elephants have large heavy bodies that they use to push down trees to reach their leaves. The ostrich has a long neck to allow its head to rise above the tops of the grass to look for predators. It has powerful legs to run fast to escape predators or to kick out to defend itself. Vultures have long, broad wings to help them glide over the grassland as they look for the remains of animals. Their beaks are hooked to help tear up any food they find.

▌ A warthog's teeth are adapted for both feeding and self-defence.

TEETH

Herbivorous grassland mammals have teeth that are adapted for cutting and grinding up food, while carnivores have large, pointed canine teeth for stabbing their prey. The warthog eats both meat and plants (omnivorous) and has teeth adapted to feed on both. Some of its teeth form tusks which it uses to defend itself from grassland predators, such as lions and leopards.

EYE ADAPTATION

Herbivorous grassland mammals such as antelopes and zebras need to see all around them as they eat. This gives them a good chance of seeing a predator approaching. They are adapted for this by having their eyes on the sides of their heads. Lions and leopards need to be able to judge distances accurately when they make their attack so that they can reach their prey. They are adapted for this by having their eyes on the front of the head. This makes the view of each eye overlap with the view of the other and allows them to judge distances better.

❙ This lion's eyes have adapted to help it to pounce on its prey quickly and accurately.

INVESTIGATE

Find out how a camel is adapted to life in a desert or how a polar bear is adapted to life in the Arctic.

PLANT ADAPTATION

The grassland habitat has wet and dry seasons. In the dry season, water is scarce. Plants such as the baobab tree only produce leaves in the wet season to reduce water loss through its leaves. The baobab is further adapted by growing small leaves that lose very little water. The baobab also has a very large trunk in which it stores water when the soil dries up.

Fossils

The first classification of living things was made by an ancient Greek called Aristotle (384–322 BCE). He was also the first to suggest that fossils were the remains of living things. Scientists who lived much later than him helped to bring the analysis of fossils into the study of evolution.

I Fossilised dinosaur bones found at a dig site in Alberta, Canada.

SEDIMENTARY ROCK

Fossils are found in sedimentary rocks. These rocks are made up of layers of tiny pieces of mud, sand and rock that have been pressed together over millions of years to form a layer of solid rock. A fossil forms from the remains of a plant or animal or from the impression it made on the ground. Fossils form in different ways.

FORMING FROM REMAINS

When a living thing dies its soft parts rot away quickly. Only the hard parts, such as bone or shell, remain. These are the parts that usually form fossils. This process only takes place if the body has fallen into sand or mud and has been quickly covered by more sand and mud. Water passes through the hard parts of the body, washing out the cells and replacing them with minerals. This makes a cast of the original part, known as a fossil.

PETRIFICATION

Another way a fossil is produced is by minerals collecting in the cells and turning a part to stone. This process is called petrification.

TRACE FOSSILS

Trace fossils are not made from part of the body of a plant or animal. Trace fossils may be an impression left in mud after a leaf has fallen onto it or the tracks across the ground left by dinosaurs. These fill with sand or mud which harden to form fossils. Trace fossils can also be the eggs left by animals or even their droppings.

I These trace fossils show the footprints of a dinosaur as it walked through its habitat over 65 million years ago.

THE JURASSIC COAST

Famous fossil collector Mary Anning (1799–1847) lived in an area now known as the Jurassic coast in Dorset, England. Millions of years ago, this whole coast was under the sea. Many dead animals that fell onto the sea bed were turned to fossils. Millions of years later, the rocks that made up the sea bed were pushed to the surface by movements in the Earth's crust.

❙ Mary Anning at work (right). Mary is holding a hammer for chipping out fossils and in the background is a cliff face where fossils can still be found.

❙ The fossil of an ichthyosaurus (fish lizard). By studying the arrangement of the bones you can work out what it may have looked like when it was alive.

FAMOUS FINDS

Mary's family gathered rocks and fossils from the Dorset cliffs and shore and sold them to visitors for a living. One day, Mary's brother Joseph discovered a large skull in a rock. Mary carefully dug out the rest of the skeleton and uncovered the fossil of a huge marine reptile named ichthyosaurus. Mary continued searching for fossils all her life. Over time, she discovered fossils of a flying reptile or pterosaur, another giant marine reptile known as a plesiosaurus and a fish called squaloraja, which provided scientists with an important link between rays and sharks.

INVESTIGATE

Find out more about ichthyosaurs, plesiosaurs and pterosaurs and describe how each was adapted to the habitat in which it lived.

The fossil record

When scientists studied the fossils in rock thoroughly, they concluded that the rocks were laid down in layers at different times in the history of the Earth.

Different layers of sedimentary rock can clearly be seen in this desert cliff face.

LAYERS IN ROCK

The layers of sedimentary rock are called strata (a single layer is a stratum). They can be seen in cliff faces, in quarries and in cuttings where the soil has been removed for roads and railways to pass through hills. Usually the layer at the bottom is the oldest and the layer at the top is the youngest.

NAMING THE LAYERS

Scientists have compared the layers of rock at different places around the world and have worked out the order in which they were all laid down. They then worked out their ages and named the layers. Different fossils are found in different layers.

Name of layer	Time when the layer was made (in millions of years ago)	Fossils of plants and animals found
Quarternary	1.6	First humans
Tertiary	65	First mammals
Cretaceous	135	End of dinosaurs
Jurassic	205	First birds, first flowering plants
Triassic	250	First dinosaurs
Permian	300	Lots of amphibians and conifer trees. End of trilobites (see p.25)
Carboniferous	355	First reptiles, first insects with wings, lots of ferns
Devonian	410	Lots of fish, first amphibians
Silurian	435	First centipedes and millipedes
Ordovician	510	First corals, first land plants
Cambrian	570	Trilobites, first molluscs
Precambrian	Before 570	Microbes and sponges

FOSSILS IN THE LAYERS

When scientists studied the fossils in the different rock layers, their discoveries about life on the Earth began. They found that most fossils, such as the first plant with a stem (Cooksonia), and arthropods called trilobites found in the older layers were not found in the younger layers. This suggests that the plants and animals that made the fossils had become extinct.

SIMILAR FEATURES

Scientists also found that some groups of fossils in the upper layers of rock had features similar to groups of fossils in the lower layers. For example, fossil conifers in upper layers have some features similar to extinct plants called cordaites in lower layers. This suggests that the plants and animals that lived long ago are related to the plants and animals that lived more recently.

I Over 20,000 different types of trilobite like this one have been identified.

CHANGE OVER TIME

Scientists further found that some groups of fossils in the upper layers are not found in the lower layers. This suggests that they formed from plants and animals that were not alive when the lower layers were made. They somehow came into existence after the lower layers had formed. As some of the groups of extinct animals seem to be related to animals alive today, for example, fossil belemnites and living squids, this suggested that some animals in the extinct group changed or evolved over time into the new animals.

I These fossil scallop shells (above) are similar to the shells of scallops that are found today (left).

INVESTIGATE

Some plants and animals are called living fossils because they are still alive today, although most of their type became extinct millions of years ago. Find out more about the horsetail and the ginkgo tree and animals known as crinoids and coelacanths.

Charles Darwin

Charles Darwin (1809–1882) was an English naturalist. He made very important discoveries about how animals and plants change over time, which became known as the theory of evolution.

TRAVELLING THE WORLD

In 1831, Darwin made a expedition around the world on a ship named the HMS *Beagle*. The voyage lasted nearly five years, and he visited South America, Australia and South Africa. Darwin was the ship's naturalist. He observed and collected a huge range of specimens of plants, animals and fossils from around the world. When Darwin finally returned home, he had begun exploring the theory that one species of living thing might develop into another species. He began research to test his theory.

ADAPTATIONS

Darwin knew that plants and animals had adaptations which helped them survive in their habitat. He had seen many adaptations on his journey, and studied the behaviour of the catasetum orchid in depth. This flower produces both male and female flowers. The male flower attracts a bee with its scent and colourful appearance. As soon as the insect enters it triggers a mechanism whereby the flower fires pollen onto the insect's back. This shocks the bee into leaving and seeking out another flower, a female flower, to deliver the pollen. This helps to ensure the continued survival of the plant.

❙ Catasetum orchid flowers ready to attract hungry bees.

❙ Charles Darwin

FOSSIL EVIDENCE

Darwin looked at the data he had collected about fossils. He saw that some animal species had died out, while there were other animal species with similar features still living in the same area. This suggested that perhaps the features of the extinct species had been passed to those that were living now.

ANIMAL BREEDING

Darwin also studied how people bred different varieties of pigeon. He saw that they selected birds with a feature they liked, such as a fantail, and bred them together to make birds with even greater fantails.

❚ Fantailed pigeons have up to 40 tail feathers while ordinary pigeons have up to 14.

DARWIN'S FINCHES

Darwin looked at the specimens of the different species of birds called finches that he had brought back from the coast of Chile and the Galapagos Islands, and found a way to link them together. He looked at their beaks and saw that the birds found on the coast of Chile had a blunt beak. This helped them pick up seeds to eat. The finches on the Galapagos Islands had a variety of beaks to allow them to eat different foods. Darwin believed these adaptations were due to some finches from Chile reaching the Galapagos Islands and producing offspring with a variety of slightly different beak shapes. Each shape helped the bird feed on different food. This meant that they did not compete for food and so all survived and produced more offspring with their different beaks. Over time, the offspring which were best adapted to collect their different kinds of foods survived and those with less adapted beaks died out. Eventually each group of birds with a different beak became a different species.

❚ Four species of Darwin's finch, showing how their beaks had evolved into different shapes.

INVESTIGATE

Follow Darwin's journey on a globe or world map. Here are some of the places he visited: Plymouth (UK), Cape Verde Islands, Salvador (Brazil), Tierra del Fuego (Chile/Argentina), Galapagos Islands (Ecuador), Sydney (Australia), Cocos Islands (Australia), Mauritius (Africa), Cape Town (South Africa), Salvador (Brazil), Plymouth (UK).

Natural selection

Charles Darwin's findings led him and fellow scientist Alfred Russel Wallace (1823–1913) to set out their Theory of Natural Selection, which describes how living things evolve. It was published in 1859 and is still used by scientists to explain how the Earth is populated by a huge variety of living things.

DARWIN'S THEORY

Darwin was trying to work out how species could change when he read a book called *An Essay on the Principle of Populations*. In it, the author Thomas Malthus claimed that a human population depended on food and if there was a famine the population would decrease. Darwin believed that the same thing could happen with other living things and set out to show how this might lead to evolution. His idea can be presented in five points.

1 An animal or plant can produce a large number of offspring. For example, frogs lay lots of eggs and a grass stalk has many seeds.

2 The size of a population of plants or animals in a habitat stays the same if the habitat does not change. A change in the habitat produces a change in the population size of the plants and animals there.

❚ Frogs produce huge numbers of eggs to make sure some will survive to become adults.

▌The size of a population of wildebeest can be reduced by effective predators such as the cheetah.

3 Even though a plant or animal produces a large number of offspring, only a few of them may survive to breed. Excluding humans, something kills off most of the offspring. There may be a lack of food so many starve, there may be lots of predators so many offspring are eaten or there may be a change in the climate, with many offspring unable to survive the change in temperature or rainfall.

4 The members of a species vary. For example, humans vary from each other in features such as hair colour or eye colour, a species of bird may have offspring with differently shaped beaks or the offspring of a plant may have flowers with different sized petals.

5 Members of a species that have the best adaptations to a change in the habitat, competition for food, the threat of predators and climate change will survive. They will also breed and pass on their adaptations to their offspring. After many generations, a successful new species evolves.

INVESTIGATE

Use books and the Internet to find out about Alfred Russel Wallace and the evidence he used to set out his theory of evolution by natural selection.

▌Thanks to natural selection, the oystercatcher bird has evolved a long beak to help it feed on buried shellfish.

Glossary

Adaptations – an inherited or acquired feature which helps a living thing to survive in its particular habitat.

Aquatic habitat – a watery habitat such as a pond, lake, river or sea.

Carnivorous – only eating meat.

Cartilage – a tough, clear material sometimes called gristle. It forms skeletons in sharks and covers the joints of bones in other vertebrates.

Cell – a tiny structure of which the bodies of all living things are made.

Cellulose – a material made by plants which is used to support all parts of their bodies.

Characteristics of life – the seven features of all living things: feeding, respiration, movement, growth, reproduction, excretion and sensitivity.

Chlorophyll – a green substance made by plants that collects energy from sunlight which plants use to make food.

Cordaites – an extinct genus of plant.

Ecologist – someone who studies the relationship between living things and their environment.

Evolve – to change from one form to another over time.

Excretion – expelling wastes from the body.

Exoskeleton – a tough case or covering that protects the body of arthropods.

Extinct – the state of a species in which all its members have died.

Fantail – a tail where a large number of the feathers spread out to form a fan shape.

Fossil – the hard remains of an animal or plant that have been left behind in rock.

Gamete – a sex cell which contains half the genes in its nucleus for making a new individual.

Generation – all the animals or plants of a certain age.

Genes – instructions in the form of a chemical called DNA (deoxyribonucleic acid) which control the works of a cell and the growth of a body.

Gills – in animals: the structures used for breathing in fish and the production of spores in fungi. In fungi: the soft, blade-like structures on the underside of the cap.

Herbivorous – only eating plants.

Invertebrate – an animal that does not have an internal skeleton made of bone or cartilage.

Life cycle – the changes that occur in an animal or plant from the beginning of its life to its death.

Microscopic – able to be seen only under a microscope.

Mould – a fungus which forms a white or coloured body on damp food such as bread.

Naturalist – a person who makes observations on the plants and animals in their habitats and records their observations.

Nucleus – a structure in the cell which contains the genes for making everything the cell needs.

Offspring – another name for an animal or plant's young.

Omnivorous – eating both plants and animals.

Parasite – a microbe or small animal that lives on or in the body of a larger animal. Microbes and some plants are also plant parasites.

Particle – a very small part of something.

Petrification – when minerals collect in the body of an animal or plant and turn it to stone.

Placenta – a disc-like structure which sticks to the uterus wall. It takes food and oxygen from a mother's blood to the embryo and takes carbon dioxide and wastes from the embryo to the mother's blood.

Plankton – a community of microscopic species of plants and animals and the eggs and larvae of larger animals.

Population – a group made up of members of the same species living in a place.

Predator – an animal that catches other animals to eat them.

Quarry – a place where rock is cut out of the ground.

Reproduction – the process in which new individuals are produced by parent plants, animals and microbes.

Respiration – the releasing of energy from food, usually by using oxygen and producing carbon dioxide.

Sedimentary rock – rock that is made up of many layers of sand, mud and rock that have been deposited there by the movement of water, ice or wind.

Over time, the layers are pressed together to form a layer of solid rock.

Sensitivity – detecting changes in the surroundings and responding to them.

Species – a group of living things which have many similarities. The males and females of a species can breed together to produce offspring which can also breed. (Note that some species can breed together, but their offspring cannot breed.)

Tentacle – a flexible arm-like structure which may be used to capture food.

Uterus – an organ in the body of most female mammals where a fertilised egg (zygote) develops into an embryo (baby).

Vertebrate – an animal that has an internal skeleton made of bone or cartilage.

Zygote – a cell made by the fusing of a male and female gamete. It contains all the genes for making a new individual and is capable of growing into one.

Index

ABOUT THIS BOOK

The aim of this book is provide information and enrichment for the topics of Classification and Evolution in the Upper Key Stage 2 UK Science Curriculum. There are five lines of scientific enquiry. By reading the book the childen are making one of them – research using secondary sources and they are also encouraged to make more on pages 13, 15, 19, 21, 23, 25 and 29. There are other lines of enquiry to be made on the following pages – Identifying, grouping and classifying: pages 5 and 11, Observing over time: page 7, Pattern-seeking: page 9. On page 27 there is a challenge to use a globe to chart Darwin's voyage.